MW01152391

I LIKE **REPTILES** AND **AMPHIBIANS!**

FUN FACTS ABOUT
TURTLES!

Carmen Bredeson

Enslow Elementary
an imprint of
Enslow Publishers, Inc.
40 Industrial Road
Box 398
Berkeley Heights, NJ 07922
USA
http://www.enslow.com

CONTENTS

WORDS TO KNOW

hatchlings (HACH lihngz)—Baby animals that are born from eggs.

prey (PRAY)—An animal that is food for another animal.

scutes (SKOOTS)—Large, hard plates that cover the shells of most turtles.

tortoises (TOR tus uz)—Some turtles that live only on land.

PARTS OF A TURTLE

shell

head

eye

tail

front foot

back foot

scute

3

WHERE DO
TURTLES
LIVE?

Green Sea Turtles

Turtles live all over the world, but not where it is very cold. Many turtles live on land close to water.

Sea turtles live in the ocean. **Tortoises** live only on land.

5

WHAT ARE TURTLE SHELLS MADE OF?

The shell of this Eastern Spiny Softshell Turtle is thick and leather-like.

Turtle shells are made of bone.

Most shells have **scutes**.

Some turtles do not have scutes.

They are called softshell turtles.

Parrot Beaked Tortoise

This Eastern Box Turtle munches on a tasty tomato.

WHAT DO TURTLES EAT?

Most turtles eat plants and small animals. Sea turtles swim fast to catch shrimp and fish. Snapping turtles hide and wait for a worm or frog to go by. Then they chomp with their HUGE jaws.

Alligator Snapping Turtle

HOW DO TURTLES EAT?

Turtles do not have teeth. Their jaws are very sharp. Turtles use their jaws and claws to rip **prey** apart. Then they swallow the pieces whole. *Gulp*.

Hawksbill Turtles like to eat coral.

An earthworm makes a quick snack for this Wood Turtle.

Eastern Box Turtle

A turtle cannot leave its shell.

HOW DO
TURTLES
STAY SAFE FROM THEIR ENEMIES?

When danger is near, some turtles hide. A land turtle can pull its head, tail, and feet into its shell. A sea turtle cannot hide in its shell. But it can swim away FAST!

ARE THE FEET OF ALL TURTLES THE SAME?

Sea turtles have feet that look like paddles. They use them to swim. Other turtles have toes with sharp claws. A big tortoise has thick feet and legs to hold up its heavy shell.

Hawksbill Turtle

14

Galapagos Tortoise

WHICH IS THE BIGGEST TURTLE?

Leatherbacks are the biggest turtles on the earth. They live in the ocean. They can grow to be six feet long.

These children came to the beach to count the eggs laid by this Leatherback Sea Turtle.

WHICH TURTLE IS THE SMALLEST?

The Speckled Cape Tortoise is the smallest. It lives in Africa. It is only four inches long when it grows up.

Speckled Cape Tortoise

HOW LONG DO
TURTLES
LIVE?

Turtles that live in freshwater can live forty years. Some sea turtles live eighty years. Giant tortoises can live more than one hundred years. Harriet, one of the oldest tortoises, lived to be 176 years old!

Here is Harriet, who was a Galapagos (guh LAH puh gohs) Tortoise.

1. A mother snapping turtle digs out a nest for her eggs.

WHAT IS THE LIFE CYCLE OF A TURTLE?

2. A few weeks later, the baby turtles crack open the eggs.

3. The hatchlings crawl away. They hide in seaweed or grass. Birds, fish, and crabs like to eat hatchlings.

4. When the young snapping turtles grow up, they will have their own babies.

LEARN MORE

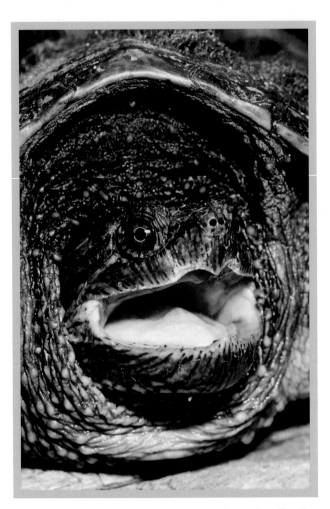

Common Snapping Turtle

BOOKS

Davies, Nicola. *One Tiny Turtle.* Cambridge, Mass.: Candlewick, 2005.

Jacobs, Francine. *Lonesome George, the Giant Tortoise.* New York: Walker & Company, 2003.

Theodorou, Rod. *Leatherback Sea Turtle.* Chicago: Heinemann Library, 2001.

Trumbauer, Lisa. *The Life Cycle of a Turtle.* Mankato, Minn.: Pebble Books, 2004.

WEB SITES

Enchanted Learning

<http://www.enchantedlearning.com/subjects/turtle/>

Kids Questions About Turtles

<http://www.turtlepuddle.org/kidspage/questions.html>

Green Sea Turtle

INDEX

Green Sea Turtle

A Note About Reptiles and Amphibians:

Amphibians can live on land or in water. Frogs, toads, and salamanders are amphibians.
Reptiles have skin covered with scales. Snakes, alligators, turtles, and lizards are reptiles.

Enslow Elementary, an imprint of Enslow Publishers, Inc.
Enslow Elementary® is a registered trademark of Enslow Publishers, Inc.

Library of Congress Cataloging-in-Publication Data

Bredeson, Carmen.
    Fun facts about turtles! / Carmen Bredeson.
        p. cm. — (I like reptiles and amphibians!)
    Includes bibliographical references and index.
    ISBN-13: 978-0-7660-2785-5
    ISBN-10: 0-7660-2785-6
    1. Turtles—Juvenile literature. I. Title.
QL666.C5B64 2007
597.92—dc22   2006035904

Printed in the United States of America

10 9 8 7 6 5 4 3 2 1

To Our Readers: We have done our best to make sure all Internet Addresses in this
book were active and appropriate when we went to press. However, the author and
the publisher have no control over and assume no liability for the material available
on those Internet sites or on other Web sites they may link to. Any comments or
suggestions can be sent by e-mail to comments@enslow.com or to the address on the
back cover.

Photo Credits: Cynthia Mead/WoodSong Nature Photography, p. 21 (top right);
© Dwight Kuhn, p. 8; © Florida Images/Alamy, p. 21 (bottom); George Grall/
NATIONAL GEOGRAPHIC IMAGE COLLECTION/Getty Images, p. 9; James
Harding/Michigan State University, p. 17; © Jim Merli/Visuals Unlimited, p. 21
(top left); © Joe McDonald/Visuals Unlimited, p. 11; © Joe & Mary Ann McDonald/
Visuals Unlimited, p. 15; © 2006 Jupiterimages Corporation, pp. 14, 22, 23;
© Lynn Stone/Animals Animals, p. 12; © NHPA/Joe Blossom, p. 6; Reinhard
Dirscherl/Alamy, p. 10; © Reinhard Dirscherl/Visuals Unlimited, pp. 4–5;
Shutterstock, pp. 1, 3, 19, 24; © Steve Maslowski/Visuals Unlimited, p. 20;
© Tony Phelps/Naturepl.com, pp. 2, 7.

Cover Photograph: © Norbert Wu/Minden Pictures

Series Science Consultant:
Raoul Bain
Herpetology Biodiversity Specialist
Center for Biodiversity and
    Conservation
American Museum of Natural History
New York, NY

Series Literacy Consultant:
Allan A. De Fina, Ph.D.
Past President of the New Jersey
    Reading Association
Professor, Department of Literacy Education
New Jersey City University
Jersey City, NJ